Fasting

GOD'S PLAN FOR HEALING FIBROID TUMORS AND OTHER MALADIES

Calvita J. Frederick

TRILOGY CHRISTIAN PUBLISHERS
TUSTIN, CA

Trilogy Christian Publishers
A Wholly Owned Subsidiary of Trinity Broadcasting Network
2442 Michelle Drive
Tustin, CA 92780

Manufactured in the United States of America

10 9 8 7 6 5 4 3 2 1

Library of Congress Cataloging-in-Publication Data is available.

ISBN: 978-1-63769-082-6

E-ISBN: 978-1-63769-083-3

Contents

Dedication

I dedicate this book to my two beautiful daughters. Thank you for your patience, your kindness, your unconditional love, and willingness to follow me to the moon and back. As your mother, I have taught you many things over the twenty-three years you have been in my life. In that same time, and with such gentleness, you both have taught me even more. There are some gifts I pray that I have given you and other God-given gifts I have helped you to cultivate. Near the top of that list, I pray that I have given you the gift of fasting. You have watched me through so many fasts and even celebrated when I was in the middle of one; you both said I do my best cooking while fasting. To that, I answer with this: When I fast, I must rely on God to do the tasting. We all know from *The Shack* that God is a Black woman who is a phenomenal cook, so I suppose it makes sense that as a cook, I shine while fasting. Jokes aside, this discipline is not one that is entered into eagerly or naturally becomes a part of your life. You must want it and work at it.

Special thanks to my daughter Samantha for editing this work. Since she was a sophomore in high school, she has been my go-to on any document proofing, including my legal documents. Thank you for your patience with me, Samantha, and by the way, I am still confused by the Oxford Comma.

To my baby girl Simone, who is so confused by commas that she can write a seven-page paper without a single one. Thank you for your expertise and creativity in helping me to decide on a title and for your vision for the book cover. Your make-up artistry and keen eye for the lighting used in my cover photo prove that the decision to send you to a performing-arts high school was money well-spent. A special thanks to you for baking the world's greatest chocolate chip cookies, which kept me going through this process.

May God bless you both, much love.

—Mom

Finally, a special thanks to my bonus daughters, Melanie Marshall and Rebekka Schaeffer, a part of our dear Oasis Church of Chicago family, where my daughters serve so faithfully. Melanie and Bekka are creative writing teachers who stepped in and provided the finishing edits when I simply could do no more. God loves you, and so do I!

Foreword

Presently, it's approximately 5 a.m. on Wednesday, July 22, 2020. We are in the middle of a pandemic, and the world is facing a crisis unlike anything we have ever seen. I am entering the third day of a long-term fast: I am not sure how long it will be; it will become clear to me at some point when I have had enough. I have been working on this book for nearly two years now, and it is still a work-in-progress. As I sit in my prayer chair in the early morning hours, I come to realize something that I have learned over and over: God's timing is not our timing. In giving us a God assignment, He also has a designated time for its completion. Rarely does it coincide with our ideas about how long the project should take.

Since the onset of COVID-19, we have been required to move through various phases of sheltering in place—a challenge to most. In this present moment, some of the restrictions have been lifted and replaced with a new normal requiring mask-wearing, frequent hand washing, and social distancing. Many of us have become accustomed to working from home, though being home has presented us with an entirely new set of challenges. Among them is the hypervisibility of the brutal and horrific images of the murders of George Floyd, Breonna Taylor, and Ahmaud Arberry. Their deaths have turned our focus to the looming presence of systemic racism, discrimination, and injustice that, like COVID-19, plagues our society.

So many things we took for granted: our jobs, the stability of our homes, our churches, schools, and the regular routine in which our lives operated. These steady elements of our lives have been ripped out from under us with little more than weeks' notice, leaving many full of fear and anxiety surrounding next steps. We've asked ourselves, "How will we survive this pandemic economically? Will the grocery stores run out of food? What are the real necessities of life?" and, "How did some of the most secure jobs in the world, healthcare providers, suddenly become the most vulnerable people on the planet?" Yet still, perhaps not out loud, we have wondered if it will be our own life lost to the dreaded unknowns of the coronavirus.

In my opinion, it's a perfect time to start a fast: many of us are home alone, filled with anxiety, questions about the future of our society, the direction of our own lives, and what tomorrow will bring. We are anxious, full of fear, overwhelmed by uncertainty, and just plain worried. Though time will undoubtedly pass, taking with it the sickness and restrictions caused by COVID-19, the sentiment and call that I offer remain.

Today, I invite you to take a journey that requires no airline tickets, no packed bags, no crowded airplanes, or long car rides. Rather, you need only decide to take a journey to seek God in a new and different way. You will find this journey will take you to places you never knew existed. You will experience new highs, new levels of understanding, joy unspeakable, and peace that passes understanding. Your creativity will be renewed, your understanding deepened, and your ability to hear God's voice seriously heightened. Peace will flood your spirit, and joy will become your new normal. Food will occupy a different space in your life as you transition from living to eat to eating to live.

It's a perfect time for a fast because you're home alone or in the presence of a few people. There are no business lunches, social events, banquets, weddings, or funerals where you will need to hide out or mumble some lame excuse about why you prefer not to eat while the food is being served. During this time, there will be no need to explain why you are not eating again and no need to look for a place where you can be alone with God. Time is on your side, and solitude is your friend. I invite you to take this exciting and life-changing journey with me. Enjoy the ride! Watch the dark circles fade from underneath your eyes and become amazed as your skin clears up. Feel the pain subside as the inflammation in your joints release from your body. You will be surprised at the increase of energy and experience sleep as you've never known. Most importantly, watch the depression lift from your spirit and the slump in your shoulders rise as you listen to God give you suggestions to resolve issues both new and those that have plagued you for years. Enjoy the ride, and then teach someone what you have learned about fasting while abiding in the presence of the Lord!

Introduction

Fasting: God's Plan for Supernatural Healing

At the suggestion of my mother, who is now a ninety-four-year-old retired registered nurse, I did my first fast. That fast lasted one day, and I was probably somewhere in my mid-twenties. Knowing my mom's weird sense of humor, I believed that I would surely die if I didn't eat for twenty-four hours and that my mother was on a secret mission designed to kill me and pass it off as a suicide. As it turns out, I was wrong on both counts.

As a nurse, my mom understood the benefits of periodic abstinence from food. Digesting food is probably the most labor-intensive function our body performs. We understand that we must not work twenty-four hours a day without sleep, and we would not dream of driving our cars year in and year out without doing some preventive maintenance; an oil change, a tune-up, or a tire rotation, etc. Yet, we never give our bodies a rest from the work necessary to digest the food we eat. I now believe and understand that fasting was designed by God for many reasons, and the healing of the body is near the top of that list.

Over the past forty years, I have completed many one-day, three-day, seven-day, fourteen-day, twenty-one-day, twenty-eight-day, and forty-day fasts. My testimony today is about a twenty-one-day fast I did in 2002 that has become a significant mark of God's work in my life.

Years before, when I was pregnant with my eldest daughter, Samantha, an ultrasound revealed that I had several fibroid tumors. At the time, I was told the fibroids were several in number, appropriate in size for my age, and would be watched throughout the pregnancy to see if they became a problem. Samantha was born in June of 1997, and it turned out the fibroids presented no problem at that time.

A few years passed, and in 2000, after the birth of my second daughter, Simone, I began to have symptoms that suggested the fibroids were becoming an issue. In my research, I found that fasting was known to cure, not shrink or manage, but cure fibroid tumors. By this time, I was a seasoned faster with more than twenty years' experience, including a fast where I had successfully been cured of psoriasis. This skin condition is thought to be incurable and therefore commonly referred to as "the heartbreak of psoriasis." I decided to try God again, and I prayed and did a twenty-one-day fast. Several months later, the symptoms returned, and my doctor suggested an outpatient procedure. The day after the procedure, Dr. Charles advised he did not know why I had the symptoms seeing that the fibroids were gone! Well, I knew why; it was God's way of providing proof to me that my healing had taken place.

About five or six years after my healing encounter, I went to an OBGYN, Dr. Louise, for a routine checkup. Dr. Louise had been my doctor decades before and had taken over for Dr. Charles, who was undergoing open-heart surgery. When Dr. Louise walked into the room, she said to me, "The last time I saw you, you were thirty-eight years old and weighed 138 pounds." After her examination, Dr. Louise commented that I had no lumps in my breasts and no fibroids. I responded that "I had none because I got rid of them with a twenty-one-day fast," to which she smiled and nodded. "Wait a minute," I said. "You are not acting as if what I just said was crazy." To that, she said, "No, I have prescribed fasts for many of my patients with fibroid tumors." The conversation continued, and Dr. Louise went on to explain that depending on factors such as how large the fibroids are, how long they have been there, and the attitude of the patient, that she believed fasting was a completely viable prescription to heal patients with fibroid tumors.

Dr. Louise then went on to say, "We do surgical removal of fibroid tumors with full knowledge that the fibroids will most likely grow back. Fasting is the way to get rid of them, but few patients will take the fasting route—they would rather go under the knife than turn their plate down for a few weeks." After that, she turned to me and said, "You should write a book."

We continued to talk about a variety of things, but before our meeting ended, Dr. Louise again insisted that I write a book on fasting and fibroid tumors. Signaling just how serious she was, she added in that she'd pull my medical records and provide the medical research to support my testimony. Well, as things go, I did not write the book, and over the course of the last several years, Dr. Louise and Dr. Charles have both died.

Despite circumstances, God has a way of getting His assignment in the forefront of your mind. In November of 2018, I heard a minister on Trinity Broadcasting Network (TBN) say, "God has given you an assignment, and you have not done as He has asked you to do." I felt the message was directed to me and promised myself to at least get started before the end of the year. Within a week, my Pastor announced from the pulpit of the church that he was looking for testimonies to be shared during Watch Night service on New Year's Eve—including ones about healing. As if that was not enough, several weeks ago, one of the Assistant Pastors at my church reinforced my assignment when he said, "Some of you are carrying ideas that can bring healing to the world." Well, they say the third time is the charm, and this was confirmation for me. So, I offer this testimony to you as the introduction of the book God revealed to me through Dr. Louise many years ago.

As an attorney with over forty years' experience, I am not easily persuaded. Rather, I have been trained to support any theory with facts to back it up and to thoroughly examine a cause of action from every conceivable direction before proceeding to take on a case. I require no less of myself as I take on this endeavor to share the power of fasting to heal fibroid tumors with you.

For those of you who are saying, "That's nice, but I don't or can't have fibroid tumors," I offer the following: I am the only adult in my immediate family who is not diabetic. My mom, dad, and sister all are or have been diabetic. That means I have a genetic predisposition for the disease, but I am convinced that the disease cannot manifest in my body because of my periodic fasting, which constantly resets my blood sugar, along with other systems in my body, including my blood pressure, my heart, lungs, kidneys, skin, etc. As previously mentioned, I also believe that I have been healed from eczema and psoriasis, a supposedly incurable skin condition, after a fourteen-day fast.

In addition, my daughters were born when I was forty-four and forty-seven years of age. During my pregnancies, I faced no issues concerning conception or fertility; I developed no gestational diabetes, no high blood pressure, and experienced no morning sickness with either pregnancy. Only two healthy, uneventful, joyous pregnancies! In fact, I was married six years and pregnant five times (the period I affectionately refer to as my bunny season, but I digress). The point is, I credit my supernaturally healthy body and the supernatural birth of my two daughters to fasting in accordance with God's Word.

If you are facing a health crisis, I challenge you to try fasting, God's plan for healing. Before you submit to surgery and allow your body to be carved up like a Thanksgiving turkey or pumped full of chemically produced drugs, turn your plate down and at least give God a chance to heal the body He created supernaturally! Join me on the God-prescribed journey that changes lives.

Prologue

Over the past fifteen years, I have struggled with the idea of writing this book and beginning this journey, and for the last eighteen months, I have struggled to complete it. Writing is a large part of what I do daily as a lawyer, and I have been told I do it reasonably well. After reading one of my Complaints, the document that starts a lawsuit, my elder brother and mentor, Attorney M, commented, "You sure know how to tell a story."

As I lamented to my long-time dear friend Annie about how hard it was to get this book done, she commented that I should get going because there is more than one book in me, and after all, it doesn't have to be a dissertation; a short book will do.

Another long-time friend Renee, an evangelist and Bible scholar, took her encouragement to another level saying, "You don't want to get to heaven and meet all the people who died because you didn't get this book written in time to help save their lives." Clearly, Renee has a way of making the truth punch you in the gut.

But I was still struggling, overworked, and just not able to find the time. "The law is a jealous mistress" is not just a saying; it's true. There'll always be another deadline facing you, or one that has just passed that you missed, and more than likely a fair share of procrastination.

Finally, in a quiet time, I felt the Lord say to me: "Just tell them what I've done for you."

Being obedient to that still small voice...here goes!

What is Fasting?

Fasting, by definition, is going without food and/or drink for a period of time. Typically, fasting is done for religious reasons and involves a person refraining from both food and drink (Esther 4:16). However, there are variations that may be done for health reasons (a juice fast, for example, where one would refrain from eating and only drink juice for a period of time).

The Oxford dictionary defines fasting as abstaining from all or some kinds of food or drink, especially as a religious observance. Some synonyms for fasting include: to abstain from food, refrain from eating, deny oneself food, go without food, go hungry, eat nothing, starve oneself, and to go on hunger strike.

Unger's Bible Dictionary explains that the word "fast" in the Bible is from the Hebrew word sum, meaning "to cover" the mouth, or from the Greek word nesteuo meaning "to abstain." For spiritual purposes, it means to go without eating and drinking. (Esther 4:16).

The Day of Atonement—also called "the Fast" (Acts 27:9)—is the only fast day commanded by God (Leviticus 23:27), though other national fast days are mentioned in the Bible. Also, personal fasts are clearly expected of Christ's disciples (Matthew 9:14-15).

Why Do We Fast?

The Bible gives examples of God's people occasionally combining fasting with their prayers so as to stir up their zeal and renew their dedication and commitment to Him. King David wrote that he "humbled [him]self with fasting" (Psalm 35:13). Fasting is a means of getting our minds back to the reality that we are not self-sufficient. Fasting helps us realize just how fragile we are and how much we depend on things beyond ourselves.

The Bible records that great men of faith such as Moses, Elijah, Daniel, Paul, and Jesus Himself fasted so that they might draw closer to God (Exodus 34:28; 1 Kings 19:8; Daniel 9:3; Daniel 10:2-3; 2 Corinthians 11:27; Matthew 4:2). Jesus knew that His true disciples, once He was no longer there in the flesh with them, would at times need to fast to regain and renew their zeal to serve Him (Mark 2:18-20).

James 4:8 (KJV) tells us, "Draw near to God and He will draw near to you." Constant prayer and occasional fasting helps us to do this. We are not called to fast to have people feel sorry for us or to think we are pious

(Matthew 6:16-18). Isaiah 58 gives both bad and good examples of fasting, contrasting wrong attitudes and actions (Isaiah 58:3-5) with the right approach of outgoing love (Isaiah 58:6-10). Daniel and Nehemiah set the example of having a repentant frame of mind (Daniel 9:3-4; Nehemiah 9:1-2). Fasting also helps us learn the lessons of the Day of Atonement: forgiveness, reconciliation to God, and the need to resist Satan and pray for the time of his removal (Revelation 20:1-3), which was portrayed in type by the Azazel goat on Atonement (Leviticus 16:20-22).

What Does the Bible Say About Fasting?

From the beginning, fasting was God's idea. The Bible makes many references to fasting, prescribing a fast as a response to various situations and circumstances life may bring. As you prepare your heart and spirit, consider these biblical references to and calls for fasting and prayer.

As an Act of Repentance

Being led by God, Jonah went into the city of Nineveh and proclaimed that God would destroy the city in forty days because of their wickedness. When the king heard of Jonah's proclamation, he ordered a fast from food and drink for man and beast accompanied by crying out to God and ceasing from evil and violence in hopes that God would change his mind. When God saw their works, He changed His mind and did not destroy Nineveh (Jonah 3:5-9).

In Joel, fasting and prayers are connected as an act of repentance ordered by God:

> *"Now therefore," says the LORD, "turn to Me with all your heart, with fasting, with weeping, and with mourning." So, rend your heart, and not your garments; return to the LORD your God, for He is gracious and merciful, slow to anger, and of great kindness. As a result, God protected them from their enemy, restored their prosperity, and He relented from doing harm.*
>
> Joel 2:12-13 (NKJV)

As a Reaction to Grief

When the men of Israel saw that Saul and his three sons were dead, they buried the bones of Saul and his sons and proclaimed a seven-day fast as their act of grief (1 Samuel 31:13).

Nehemiah also turned to fasting and prayer as an expression of his grief about the conditions facing by the Jews and Jerusalem: "So it was, when I heard these words, that I sat down and wept, and mourned for many days; I was fasting and praying before the God of heaven" (Nehemiah 1:4, NKJV).

When God's Help Is Needed

When King Jehoshaphat learned that a great army was coming against Judah and Jerusalem, and he was very afraid, he proclaimed a fast. "And Jehoshaphat feared, and set himself to seek the LORD, and proclaimed a fast throughout all Judah. So, Judah gathered together to ask help from the LORD; and from all the cities of Judah they came to seek the LORD" (2 Chronicles 20:3-4, KJV).

Your Attitude About the Fast

The Bible also gives instructions about the attitude and approach we should have in fasting. Jesus warned about hypocritical fasting, trying to show off or make others feel sorry for us.

> And when you fast, do not look gloomy like the hypocrites, for they disfigure their faces that their fasting may be seen by others. Truly, I say to you, they have received their reward. But when you fast, anoint your head and wash your face, that your fasting may not be seen by others but by your Father who is in secret. And your Father who sees in secret will reward you.
>
> Matthew 6:16-18 (ESV)

To Get Closer to God

Although it is not commanded that we fast in the Bible, it is certainly suggested as a way to get closer to God and to grow in our relationship with Him. The Bible presents fasting as a discipline that is good, fruitful, profitable, rewarding, and beneficial. It is a way to show God and to prove to ourselves that we are serious about a certain situation. Fasting turns our focus away from the world and its problems and places it on God. It quiets the noise both from the world around us and that of the fear, anxiety, and confusion raging within our own inner spirit. It helps us to gain a new perspective and expands our reliance on God.

In the New Testament, Anna, the prophetess, is described as serving God day and night with fasting and prayers (Luke 2:37). We read that John the Baptist taught his disciples to fast, and Jesus Christ said His disciples would fast after His death (Mark 2:18-20).

Paul and Barnabas prayed and fasted when they ordained elders in the church (Acts 14:23). In fact, Paul said his sacrifice and service to the church was often "in labors, in sleeplessness, in fastings" (2 Corinthians 6:5). And Jesus Christ fasted forty days and nights before facing Satan in an epic battle of spiritual will (Matthew 4:2).

As an Act of Worship

While they were worshiping the Lord and fasting, the Holy Spirit said, "Set apart for me Barnabas and Saul for the work to which I have called them" (Acts 13:2).

To Draw Closer to God and Renew Our Zeal to Serve Him

The Bible records that great men of faith such as Moses fasted: "And he was there with the Lord forty days and forty nights; he did neither eat bread nor drink water. And he wrote upon the tables the words of the covenant, the ten commandments" (Exodus 34:28, KJV).

Elijah, "And he arose, and did eat and drink, and sent in the strength of that meat forty days and forty nights unto Horeb the mount of God" (1 Kings 19:8, KJV); Daniel, "And I set my face unto the Lord God, to seek by prayer and supplications, with fasting, and sackcloth, and ashes" (Daniel 9:3, KJV). "In those days I Daniel was mourning three full weeks. I ate no pleasant bread, neither came flesh nor wine in my mouth, neither did I anoint myself at all, till three whole weeks were fulfilled" (Daniel 10:2-3, KJV).

Paul, "In weariness and painfulness, in watching often, in hunger and thirst, in fastings often, in cold and nakedness" (2 Corinthians 11:27, KJV); and Jesus Himself fasted so that they might draw closer to God, "And when he had fasted forty days and forty nights, he was afterward a hungered" (Matthew 4:2, KJV).

Jesus knew that His true disciples, once He was no longer there in the flesh with them, at times would need to fast to regain and renew their zeal to serve Him.

> And the disciples of John and of the Pharisees used to fast: and they come and say unto him, why do the disciples of John and of the Pharisees fast, but they disciples fast not? And Jesus said unto them, Can the children of the bridechamber fast, while the bridegroom is with them, they cannot fast. But the days will come, when the bridegroom shall be taken away from them, and then shall they fast in those days.
>
> Mark 2:18-20 (KJV)

Also, as mentioned before, in the book of James, the Bible tells us, "Draw near to God and He will draw near to you" (James 4:8, KJV).

To Humble Oneself Before God

Fasting is used by Ezra, the scribe as he chronicles his journey to Jerusalem: "Then I proclaimed a fast there, at the river of Ahava, that we might afflict ourselves before God, to seek of him a right way for us, and for our little ones, and for all our substance" (Ezra 8: 21, KJV). And in Psalm, by David, when he proclaimed: "But as for me, when they were sick, my clothing was sackcloth; I humbled my soul with fasting" (Psalm 35:13, KJV); and again by David, "When I wept, and chastened my soul with fasting, that was to my reproach" (Psalm 69:10, KJV).

As for Healing

Interestingly, it does not appear that the Bible directly proclaims fasting as a method to obtain healing of a condition of the human body. Rather, the Bible is full of references where miraculous healing took place as a result of faith in God to answer prayers.

There are many references that advise us to pray for healing: "Is anyone among you sick? Let him call for the elders of the church, and let them pray over him, anointing him with oil in the name of the Lord" (James 5:14, KJV). Or, "If my people, which are called by my name, shall humble themselves, and pray, and seek my face, and turn from their wicked ways, then will I hear from heaven, forgive their sin, and heal their land" (2 Chronicles 7:14, KJV).

Just recently, I heard one of my favorite Pastors Jentzen Franklin, say, "Fasting without prayer is just a diet...a cruel diet." And he is right. Therefore, I believe it is not a stretch to find biblical support for the idea that God intended us to use fasting and prayer to seek His hand to heal our infirmities. The implication is certainly there, and I have found Him faithful in my fasting journeys, specifically asking for healing certain conditions in my body.

In Luke 8:43-48, the Bible tells of the faith of a woman who had been ill for many years with a bleeding disorder. Her many efforts and trips to the doctor had proved fruitless, and she was out of money necessary to pay for any more treatments. The woman with the issue of blood surmised that Jesus had healing in His wings and that if she could touch any part of Him (even the hem of His garment) that His grace would meet her faith, and she would be healed. Although this passage mentions neither prayer nor fasting, it does strongly suggest to me that God honors our faith. Taken a step further, I read this passage and have found in my life that even if my faith is ill-placed, my actions are somewhat ridiculous (stop eating when you are sick?), defying logic and/or reason, that if I acknowledge that I need God's help, desperately seek His intervention, draw near to Him, believe in His power, turn down my plate and focus on Him, He simply has to come. And come He will.

The Fast for Improper Reasons

The Bible cautions against fasting for the wrong reasons, some of which are: to look holy and more spiritual than others. In Matthew 6:16-18 (NIV), we are told:

> When you fast, do not look somber as the hypocrites do, for they disfigure their faces to show men they are fasting. I tell you the

> truth, they have received their reward in full. But when you fast, put oil on your head and wash your face, so that it will not be obvious to men that you are fasting, but only to your Father, who is unseen; and your Father, who sees what is done in secret, will reward you.

Christian Fasting

For Christians, fasting is to be done in a spirit of humility and with a joyful attitude. The work required for our bodies to digest food is a labor-intensive, all-consuming process. Even though we are not consciously aware of the process of digesting food, once we enter the fasting zone, one thing becomes clear. Our ability to focus on our prayer life is greatly enhanced. Our attention span is lengthened, our conversations with God become more frequent, and His presence and guidance are easier to discern.

Am I suggesting that fasting is a foolproof, get-healed-quick, guaranteed method to get God to do what you want? Certainly not. Rest assured, a fast is not easy, even for those of us who are seasoned fasters, having engaged in the discipline for years. Each fast carries with it its own challenges. Headaches are not uncommon, and there will undoubtedly be dinners, parties, weddings, holidays, and funerals during your fast, where food has never looked so good. Might I add the problem of those around you determined to knock you off course by chowing down in front of you and waving their cheeseburger, fried fish, or brownie under your nose? But these challenges are no different, greater, or smaller than any other challenge you have faced or will face in life: taking money that is not yours, doing drugs, engaging in illicit sexual relationships, or cheating on your taxes. When you are all in and have made up your mind, no challenge that Satan brings is too great for you.

That being said, you will find that sometimes, no matter how much you want to, you simply can't get through this particular fast. That happens, so don't beat yourself up. Eat and try it again later.

My Personal Experience

Although the focus of this book is on fasting as His tool for healing, I've oft time used fasting under other circumstances. For example, when I faced a giant corporation in a legal battle and knew I had to go before a biased judge, I turned to fasting. When I've faced problems for which I had no answer, fasting provided the clarity and understanding I needed to approach the situations. And perhaps most relatable, when my appetite and/or my weight were out of control, fasting has called me back to my health and wellbeing.

Fasting: Getting God's Attention

Jesus Heals a Boy with a Demon

Throughout the gospels, we learn of the time Jesus heals the boy with a demon (Mark 9:14-29; Luke 9:37-42; and Luke 17:5-10). This story is of particular relevance when it comes to the notion of fasting to get God's attention because of the explicit direction to turn down one's plate. More specifically, I want to share with you Matthew 17:19-21 (KJV), which reads,

> Then came the disciples to Jesus apart, and said, why could not we cast him out? And Jesus said unto them, Because of your unbelief: for verily I say unto you, if ye have faith as a grain of mustard seed, ye shall say unto this mountain, remove hence to yonder place; and it shall remove; and nothing shall be impos-

> sible unto you. Howbeit this kind goeth not out but by *prayer and fasting*.
>
> (emphasis added)

I am most grateful for the times I fasted because many times, I was desperate for an answer or intervention from God. The above scripture points us in that direction. Jesus' disciples found themselves faced with a huge challenge after an unsuccessful attempt to remove a demon from a boy. What they failed to realize is that some obstacles are only overcome by *fasting and prayer.* Turning your plate down, especially for an extended period of time, is a desperate move. It says, "I need a miracle, and I believe God's Word when it says some things require more than prayer alone." Understanding "God is not a man that He should lie," I believe that He will do what He promises He will do (Numbers 23:19).

Similar to the disciples, I've faced many of life's challenges. Reflecting on my family life, my health, and my career, I have consistently needed to call on and get God's attention when facing various issues. Though the examples of God's intervention in my life are many, in this chapter, I highlight a few I think you'll find particularly compelling.

Family Life Challenges

In one especially trying instance, I had to suddenly and unexpectedly move from my home of twenty-plus years due to reasons related to self-employment. Never mind that this was a house that I had built from the ground up while single, the house where I was married, where I lived when both of my daughters were born, and that contained a host of happy memories. Although I had no money, two children, a dog, and nowhere to go, I did have my faith. Knowing that only God could get me through this episode, I turned my plate down, began to fast, and the Lord began to move. First, the time I had been given to complete the move kept getting extended. Every time I thought we were at the end of the rope, a suggestion was made, many times coming from the enemy, that allowed another two, three, or seven days to the deadline. Second, friends showed up not only to lend a hand but were filled with helpful suggestions, including leading me to the greatest movers in the world who became family to me in my time of need. Third, a dear friend who knew what I was facing called and offered me temporary housing, apologizing that it was not what I was used to, but it was available to me if I wanted or needed it. She didn't stop there but paid the rent for me for the next three months. As I began the overwhelming chore of sorting through and packing up twenty years of my life, I found myself with supernatural energy, financial provision, the support of people around me, and most importantly, an overwhelming sense of peace, relief, and even excitement as

I closed one painful chapter and opened a new one. The move took days from packing to completion, and on several of those days, I became aware that I didn't even stop for water (which I do not recommend). We stayed in the temporary housing provided by my dear friend, and within four months, God blessed us with a historic home built by Frank Lloyd Wright in an affluent suburb: a better home than the one I was called to leave.

I share my testimonies in the different avenues of my life as encouragement to you, whether you are well on your way to fasting for healing or still on the fence.

As previously mentioned, I have been self-employed for many decades. In my business, I have no regular clients or assignments that pay me monthly. Rather, my income is based upon retainer fees (i.e., down payments from which I can draw) new business, sent by the Lord, and cases that I am able to settle. Many of the cases I take are on a contingency fee basis, meaning I only get paid when and if I win. I am sure that many of you who have a job are thinking, I could never live like this, the uncertainty of income facing me literally every month. To you, I say, I could never operate in a job where I am told each day what to do, even if it goes against my beliefs of what is right, wrong, or necessary; I am mentally and or emotionally abused by a supervisor, co-worker or boss who dislikes and or attacks me for reasons I cannot control, like my sex, race, or religious beliefs, and who has the ability to end my job/career with no notice simply because they have the power to do so. For those of you, who like me, are self-employed, for some reason, we are better equipped to handle the uncertainly of finances rather than the requirements of office politics. It all depends on how you are wired and which uncertainties are the least offensive to you. I tried a corporate assignment, and although I liked the regular paycheck and benefits, the politics of it all were giving me an ulcer, as confirmed by my doctor. I, therefore, had to find an alternative, which was self-employment.

Please don't think that I am for one moment suggesting that self-employment with its uncertainty of income is easy or for everyone. It is not. But fasting has been the method through which I have become comfortable in this arena of self-employment, another of life's uncertainties for me.

One of my favorite scriptures in this area is God will supply all of your needs according to His riches in glory through Christ Jesus. In so many instances over the years when I had no money and none on the horizon, as far as I knew, fasting was my only choice. Likewise, the instances of how God came through, time after time after time, are so numerous, I have forgotten those that I didn't write down. New clients came out the woodwork, referred by people whose names I didn't even know or remember, opposing counsel called and advised their client wanted a quick settlement, an old bill that I had given up on got paid, a rebate or stimulus check not only came but was many times greater than expected, or someone simply called and said God said to bless you and sent me thousands of dollars. Although I may not remember the exact details, this I do remember: *God has always come through,* and this is what sticks with me when I face this situation.

On more than one occasion, I have had to make quick changes in where my daughters went to school. In one instance, my younger daughter, who was a freshman in high school at the time, was being bullied by a teacher. The administration of the school refused for a time to even discuss the matter with me. Finally, a well-heeled donor to the school, who had become a friend of the family, made a call on my behalf. As a result, a meeting was set with several of the school administrators, in which we would discuss the bullying incidents. I was notified that I would be allowed to bring one person besides myself to the meeting. I chose my dear friend Billy, whom I had known for decades, long before the girls were born. Billy was an optimal choice, seeing as we were not only part of the same spiritual community, but he was also a neighbor and former client of mine as well. I knew Billy to be level-headed and objective. His faith in God and business experience sharpened his abilities to mediate conflict. After the meeting, Billy advised me to get my daughter out of that school immediately. I did, but with nowhere for her to go upon her departure.

The only option, at least for that semester, was home schooling. Despite having certifications to teach high school history, I had neither the time nor the patience to take on this gargantuan task. After spending several days filled with fear and frustration, I turned down my plate again and began to pray fervently about my daughter's education. I found my scriptures in the KJV, paraphrased them, and prayed them throughout the day: No weapon formed against me will prosper; (Isaiah 54:17). God is able to do exceedingly abundantly above all we can ask think or imagine; (Ephesians 3:20-21). Behold, I have set before you an open door which no man can close; (Revelation 3:8). You have not because you ask not, ask and it shall be given, seek and you shall find, knock and the door will be opened (Matthew 7:7).

As I searched for options and found few, I learned of the Chicago Academy for the Arts (hereafter CAA), a highly rated performing-arts high school in Chicago. At her previous school, both of my daughters were heavily involved in the school's choirs, participating in statewide competitions, taking private voice lessons, commanding solos, and leads throughout their respective tenures. They also cultivated their acting skills through participation in school musicals, bringing together their love of singing and acting with their ongoing training in dance.

This, coupled with the fact that both my daughters had trained in dance from the age of three, made a strong case for CAA as a potential fit for my younger daughter's high school career. On a more logistical level, CAA was one of few schools in our city that accepted mid-year transfers.

After contacting the school, I was directed to the Illinois Home Schooling Association, where I was advised to enroll my daughter in the home-schooling program while she went through the process of auditioning and shadowing at CAA for the following semester.

One day while talking with Billy, he asked if I knew of his wife's credentials. I soon learned that she was a Northwestern grad, a whiz in English and Math, and was open to homeschooling my daughter during the interim period while we waited to hear the results of her audition.

Suffice it to say, my daughter was accepted into CAA, and although the scholarship money was gone for the remainder of her freshman year, leaving me with a hefty tuition bill, she successfully graduated three and a half years later. Not only that, but she was recruited by a performing arts college and given a full scholarship to attend. God closes one door and opens a bigger and better one if we can just believe.

Health Challenges: Diverting Major Diagnoses

Many of my fasts began in response to a particular illness: the fibroid tumor being the most notable. I have been given a number of major diagnoses such as eczema, psoriasis, diverticulitis, high blood sugar, and the need for a root canal, to name a few. I have also experienced more common ailments such as colds, toothaches, and other episodes of inflammation. For many of these, I fasted, and of course, prayed. Seeing that you're more than likely still reading to hear the outcome of these fasts, here they are: The eczema and psoriasis never came back; the diverticulitis, infection, and/or inflammation in the intestines, was resolved; my blood sugar levels adjusted, and I remain free of diabetes.[1] My colds withered away, and I never submitted to a root canal for my painful toothache. Though, in the case of my tooth, even though the pain subsided, I lost that tooth four years later.

Conception, Pregnancies, and Deliveries

Though mentioned in earlier chapters, I was able to conceive, carry to term, and deliver two beautiful, healthy girls. Their births came at a time when conventional wisdom, along with a number of well-meaning loved ones, suggested that my age would almost certainly create a number of complications—if not all-out disasters. I don't mean to sound flippant, but to these cautions, I turned a deaf ear, seeking instead to ask God for His direction. What I am trying to convey is that if God has placed a desire in your heart (and God takes our desires seriously), then you may have to shut out conventional wisdom. Our health providers, family, and friends mean well, but their opinions are sometimes based largely on fear. One helpful tool I used in overcoming that fear was a book entitled *Supernatural Childbirth: Experiencing the Promises of God Concerning Conception and Delivery.*[2]

Although I cannot prove it, I firmly believe that at the time of conception with each of my daughters, my body was in a supernatural state of health. I attribute this to the fact that my decisions to attempt motherhood at an advanced age were preceded by much fasting and prayer (not that I was fasting during my pregnancies!). Nevertheless, I return to my unwavering belief in capturing God's attention by way of fasting! I share these health experiences, large and small, along with my journey to joyous motherhood to emphasize that God's Word is true. You need faith only the size of a mustard seed to step into your God-given authority.

My Career Challenges

Throughout my time as a lawyer, I have handled many cases, including personal injury, products liability, and employment discrimination. I have fought major corporations (including Fortune 500),[3] represented by large well-known, and well-staffed law firms, and won. When facing these cases, which I like to call "Goliath's," I have on many occasions submitted myself to God through fasting and prayer. It is in this posture that I gain access to the throne of grace and get God's ear. I can just imagine Him saying, "Oh, she's turned her plate down again; it must be serious. I must go and see what she wants this time, lest the child starves herself to death." This is not to say I always get exactly what I want because God answers in three ways: yes, no, and wait. While I do get some slam dunk victories, I have also been instructed by the Lord to withdraw from cases. But even in these moments of concession, God grants me peace in His decision and, at times, an understanding of why things went the way they did.

In one case, I based a claim of wrongful death on the fact that my client, after suffering a heart attack, was placed on a restriction from strenuous activities, such as sports. Soon after, he returned to work and, one day, fell dead from a subsequent heart attack while he was standing still and doing absolutely nothing at the time. When I sought the opinion of the doctor who had provided the strenuous activity restriction, it turned out that the doctor's medical license had been revoked, and he had left the country. While this could have been a hard hit for my case, it was of no consequence because, miraculously, the company was intent on settling the case quickly. The judge presiding over the settlement conference became my proponent, viewing the other side's liability as substantial. A friend and colleague of mine with whom I later discussed this case looked at me in amazement and said, "Not only do I *not* understand why they paid, I'm trying to understand what your theory of liability was in the first place."

That case settled for six figures after several lawyers before me had turned it down. One well-known firm, with whom I'd tried to refer the case, turned it down as having no merit. They further stated that I lacked the experience and expertise necessary to properly evaluate and/or handle this type of case. In my fasting and prayer time, God spoke to me and said, "I didn't give you this case to have you give it away. I will provide for you the wisdom needed." Just like He promised, God was faithful. This case was the first in a long line of *David vs. Goliath* cases that I have won, depending on God and fasting and praying. God repeatedly gives me favor with judges, with my clients, and sometimes even with opposing counsel.

Standing on Biblical Truth

When fasting and praying about the challenges life throws my way, I have identified and memorized a number of scriptures I speak out loud on a regular basis, including during a fast. These are particularly helpful when fear is trying to overtake me.

1. Numbers 23:19 (KJV)
   "God is not man, that He should lie, or a son of man, that He should change His mind. Has He said, and will He not do it? Or has He spoken, and will He not fulfill it?"

2. 1 John 4:4 (KJV)
   "Ye are of God, little children, and have overcome them: because greater is He that is in you, than He that is in the world."

3. 2 Timothy 1:7 (KJV)
   "God has not given us a spirit of fear, but of power, and of love, and of a sound mind."

4. Isaiah 54:17 (KJV)
   "No weapon that is formed against thee shall prosper; and every tongue that shall rise against thee in judgment thou shalt condemn. This is the heritage of the servants of the LORD, and their righteousness is of me, saith the LORD."

5. Psalm 138:7-8 (KJV)
   "Though I walk in the midst of trouble, thou wilt revive me: thou shalt stretch forth thine hand against the wrath of mine enemies, and thy right hand shall save me. The LORD will perfect that which concerneth me: thy mercy, O LORD, endureth forever: forsake not the works of thine own hands."

6. Psalm 32:8 (KJV)
   "I will instruct thee and teach thee in the way which thou shalt go: I will guide thee with mine eye."

7. Luke 12:11-12 (KJV)
   "And when they bring you unto the synagogues, and unto magistrates, and powers, take ye no thought how or what thing ye shall answer, or what ye shall say: For the Holy Ghost shall teach you in the same hour what ye ought to say."

The Word can be used as a shield and a sword, rendering you infallible to the enemy's attacks. I suggest that you search the Word for passages that speak to your needs, but these are a few that I have found to be powerful. We prepare for war in a time of peace. That said, it is good to commit Scripture to memory in the now so that they are readily available in your time of need, tucked away in your heart, and etched in your mind. Just like a seasoned driver effortlessly grabs his keys and goes, so too should those portions of God's Word be on autopilot in your spirit.

Types of Fast

The world often refers to fasting as a diet plan or intermittent fasting. It recognizes the benefits of fasting and lists many. Some of these benefits include boosting metabolism, generating energy, obtaining health benefits, and losing weight without the need for measuring food and changing your diet. Fasting is defined by Wikipedia as "abstinence from food and drink for a specified period of time." A distinction is made between fasting and starving yourself, which fasting is not. The world recognizes the thousands of years the discipline of fasting has been around, credits this to the spiritual roots of fasting, and its ties to many religions as faith-based rituals or requirements.

Several types of fasts are suggested, including:

The Complete Fast

This fast relies solely on water and no food of any kind at any time during the period. It is the hardest fast to do and produces the greatest result. My understanding of fasting allows for herbal tea to be consumed during any fast. When I have sought to do what I consider a complete fast for me, I have always allowed for a glass of orange or apple juice if I felt weak.

The Master Cleanse

This fast consists of a specially made lemonade (distilled water, cayenne pepper, maple syrup, and lemon or lime juice), salt water flush, and laxatives and lasts for a period of at least ten days. Only the lemonade, plain water, and herbal tea are consumed, so the Master Cleanse is referred to as the lemonade diet, which produces rapid weight loss in a short period of time. I am a heavy proponent of this plan as the ingredients in the lemonade provide many of the vitamins, minerals, and nutrients our body needs while abstaining from food. I also find that consumption of this lemonade while fasting eliminates the feeling of hunger and makes the fast doable. I discuss the ingredients contained in the lemonade and the health benefits in the next chapter.

Intermittent Fasting

Intermittent fasting is a catch-all phrase that encompasses most of the other types of fasting. It is an on-again, off-again method of fasting where the abstention from food lasts anywhere from fourteen to thirty-six hours. I have a friend who has practiced this type of fasting for years: each week, he fasts from Sunday night to Tuesday at noon. He is very disciplined.

Restricted Hours for Eating

Time-restricted fasting requires you to abstain from eating for a certain number of hours or time span each day. A likely plan would have you eat for twelve hours and abstain for twelve hours. For example, during Ramadan, the Muslim community does not eat between sunrise and sunset, roughly 6 a.m.–7 p.m. After 7 p.m., they can eat as much as they want of any healthy foods they choose. This type of fasting, which requires the abstention of food from sunrise to sunset and then allows for a huge and healthy meal, is palatable to many people new to fasting or to those who have difficulty with the concept of not eating for a full day.

16/8 Fast

16/8 fasting is another type of time-restricted fasting where one abstains for sixteen hours and eats for eight hours a day.

Alternate Day Fasting

Alternate day fasting has you eat a normal calorie intake (2000 calories) one day and then consume a severely restricted amount of food (only 500 calories) the following day. This type of fasting is considered more difficult and is usually not recommended as a long-term fast.

The 5:2 Fast

The 5:2 is much like the alternative day fasting and allows you to normally eat for five days and then restrict your calorie intake to 500-600 calories for two days.

The Warrior Diet

The Warrior diet allows one to eat a well-balanced meal in the evening after restricting your diet during the earlier part of the day to fruits and vegetables.

The Daniel Fast

Finally, the Daniel Fast is taken straight from the book of Daniel in the Bible. It is usually a twenty-one-day fast wherein one eats fruits, vegetables, and other whole foods, avoiding meat, dairy, un-sprouted grains, sweets, coffee, and alcohol while focusing on one's relationship with God.

"In those days, I Daniel was mourning three full weeks. I ate no pleasant bread, neither came flesh or wine in my mouth..." (Daniel 10:2-3, KJV).

To find more about different types of fasting, please refer to Dr. AXE's website "Food and Medicine," an article written by Kissairis Munoz (January 10, 2018).

Natural Benefits of Fasting

Weight Loss

Of course, the number one benefit is weight loss. Various studies around the country have supported the idea that fasting produces loss of body weight and body fat. The loss of inches and belly fat can also be expected, along with a reduction in inflammation levels and shrinkage of the waistline, as per one study conducted in Southern California in 2015.[4]

Increasing the Human Growth Hormone

Although the human growth hormone (HGH) is naturally produced by the body, its production is increased by fasting. Because HGH is necessary for burning fat, fasting can assist with treating obesity and improving workouts by burning fat while building lean muscle mass.

Because fasting promotes the production of HGH and boosts fat burning while increasing lean muscle mass, fasting is particularly good for athletes.

Decreasing the Hunger Hormone

Ghrelin, known as the hunger hormone, is responsible for telling your body when it is hungry. Although ghrelin levels can be increased by dieting, fasting is known to normalize the level of this hormone. The long-term effect of the reduction in the production of this hormone will help your body to realize when it is really hungry rather than eating just because it is dinner time.

Reduction of Bad Cholesterol

Intermittent fasting is also known to reduce the bad cholesterol levels in your body by decreasing the production of triglycerides without affecting the good cholesterol level. This process helps reduce the risks of heart disease.

Increase in Longevity

Although not proven in humans, animal studies suggest that intermittent fasting may increase longevity.

Benefits for Diabetics

The World Journal of Diabetes has conducted several studies that have found that;

(1) intermittent fasting in adults with Type 2 diabetes improved key markers, including weight loss and glucose levels;
(2) intermittent fasting was as effective as restricting your caloric intake in reducing visceral fat mass, fasting insulin, and insulin resistance;
(3) intermittent fasting can help normalize things if you're struggling with insulin sensitivity or pre-diabetes.[5]

As with any discipline, the scientific world recognizes that fasting is not for everyone. Particularly at risk are those who are insulin-dependent, nursing mothers, and pregnant women.

A recent New York Times article reviewed intermittent fasting as a type of diet. The writer, who suffered from Type 1 diabetes, found the eating plan not only doable but also pleasant for a number of reasons:

First, by limiting the hours a day he ate (he used eight hours between 11 a.m. and 7 p.m.), his concentration was more about when he was eating than what he was eating. He could eat a lot more of what he loved and was freed from not having to count calories.

Second, he enjoyed what he called the Zen-like feeling that accompanied the intermittent fasting and freed him from what he termed his "mental load," or the time he spent thinking about diabetes and what to eat.

Third, because the plan he set for himself required two meals a day and a small snack in between, he had to take less insulin.

Fourth he liked the feeling of being in control of his body.

Fifth, he found the intermittent fasting plan easy to adopt.

Sixth, the benefits of intermittent fasting were numerous and included reduced body weight, reduced body fat, reduced cholesterol, improved glucose levels, reduced liver fat, increased endurance, and better motor coordination.

Seventh, he experienced better sleeping, and both his sleep drive increased, and the sleep he experienced was much better.

Eighth, since fasting reduces caloric intake, it is believed to increase the life span of even healthy people, which is also believed to decrease the rate of heart disease and may even prevent the reoccurrence of breast cancer.[6]

Who Should Fast?

Everyone should, at some time in their life and for any length of time, go on a fast. Although it is understood that fasting, as the abstention from all food, may not be an alternative for people on certain kinds of medication (like insulin-dependent diabetics or those with heart conditions and high blood pressure), they are certainly not left on their own. There are certain physician groups who specialize in holistic medicine that may be able to assist and oversee a fast for those medically challenged who want to try a fast. Indeed, certain people with chronic illness have successfully used the fast to attack and experience healing from these very chronic conditions.

I say everyone should fast because one of the benefits of abstaining from food for a period of time is to grow into a closer relationship with God. It sounds cliché, and it's hard to explain, but there is a place you go and a feeling you experience, unlike anything you have done before. It's a quiet space, a special place where God shows Himself to you in a way few people get to see. It's as if you get invited to a private club, a club where you are aware of God and know that He's aware of you. You get to speak to God in an intimate and personal one-on-one level, and more importantly, you enter into a place where you can hear from God clearly. There's no interference or distractions (and the longer you fast, within reason), the more you come to realize how distracting food is.

You know how difficult it can sometimes be to get in and stay in an atmosphere of prayer. You start, and you drift off. Forgetting where you are, and so you start over and try again only to realize once again, your thoughts and mind have drifted far away from the conversation you were trying to have with God. Well, there is something about talking to God while fasting that greatly improves your attention span. Even though we know fasting does not change God, there does seem to be something about that change in you that appears or feels like it brings about a change in God.

Let me explain it this way: I am a mom, and on any given day, I see my daughter go out of her way to please me. For example, she cooks my breakfast, cleans her room, offers to do my laundry, and there is absolutely nothing she is trying to get from me. It causes me to want to do something nice for her. Let me get a good report from her teacher about how well she performed in class or how she went to the aid of another student; you can best believe she is going to get a fantastic dinner or her choice of fast food that night, a trip to the movies, nail salon or whatever else her heart desires.

Well, it works the same way with God. You decide to turn your plate down in an effort to deepen your relationship with God; you can bet you get God's attention at a different level. And it is His nature to want to bless us anyway for any or no reason, just because He is God, and God is good. Just imagine the effect that denying yourself your most basic need, food, and humbling your very soul with fasting and prayer will have on God.

By fasting, you are saying to our Father that you want more of Him than just the entry-level relationship; you desire more of Him, you want to go deeper in your relationship with Him and get to know more about Him. And not only do you want more, but you are also willing to go to great lengths, the very lengths He ordained as the pathway to answered prayer for the most difficult of situations and this deeper relationship with our Father.

And it's not just to get more things, because it's unlikely you will be able to deny your most basic need, for a new dress. Just the idea of going without food for an extended period of time is something you wouldn't do unless you are at or near the point of desperation and you have a need for a supernatural intervention from

God, like a miraculous healing in your body; like for removal of a fibroid tumor.

So, the answer to the question who should fast: if you are still reading this far into this book...I think it is you!

Why Does Fasting Work?

In the Spiritual

First, fasting works simply because God *said* it would. "This kind does not go out except by prayer and fasting" (Matthew 17:21, WEB).

Fasting was ordained by God and is specifically mentioned as a petition to Him when the need is great and nothing else has worked. In the biblical reference above, Jesus spoke those words in response to the disciples' question as to why they could not pray and heal the young boy who was possessed by demons and described as a lunatic. The disciples had tried to heal the lad but to no avail. Jesus was approached and rebuked the devil, and the devil departed from the boy. In His answer, Jesus was saying there are certain times when a regular, everyday prayer will not do...you must go deeper...you must assume a posture that says to God we need more and know that sometimes asking big of

God requires more from us (Matthew 17:19-20). It is as if we must assume the position. For supernatural healing, we must pray a supernatural prayer. And according to God's Word, the position for praying a supernatural prayer is the position you get into when you decide to combine your prayer with a fast and enter what I call the fasting zone.

By placing yourself in the *fasting zone*, you are saying several things to God:

1. I have read Your Word;
2. I understand Your Word to instruct me to approach You from a different position when I want You to move supernaturally on my behalf and do something really big;
3. I believe You will do as You promised me in Your Word;
4. I trust that I will not be hurt when I follow the guidelines set out in Your Word; and
5. I trust You to answer my prayer in the best way, even if it is not in the exact manner that I seek or expect.

You see, "God is not a man that he should lie;" (Numbers 23:19, KJV). He said it, I believe it, and it is so.

In the Natural

Not surprisingly, the world has caught on to God's plan of fasting and studied it from a holistic perspective. God made man in His image, and in so doing, He designed our bodies with the absolute ability to heal themselves. But our bodies never get the chance or the time to heal themselves because digesting food is such a labor-intensive, 24/7 activity. Because we eat from three to six meals a day, most each and every day, our bodies never get a rest from digesting food and the time to perform preventive maintenance. The maintenance our bodies need is not unlike a tune-up for your car or what a school does during the summer months when the building is closed and students are out on break.

A tune-up is not done when your car breaks down; that's a repair. Rather a tune-up is designed to take place on a regular basis to *prevent* a breakdown. You change the oil so that the engine has good quality oil to keep its parts clean, lubricated, and in good working order. You rotate the tires so that they will wear evenly and last longer, and you look for any nails or worn spots in order to repair them before they cause a flat tire. You change the air filter so that the parts of your engine that need to breathe in order to run properly are not obstructed by dirt and dust.

While schools are closed, they paint the walls, deep clean, service the HVAC systems, and make necessary repairs so that the school is in proper and functioning order. Without this annual upkeep, schools run the risk of a breakdown during the school year or an outbreak of an illness and disease.

When do we ever give our *bodies* a tune-up or perform preventive maintenance? For most of us: Never! Even when we take what we call a "vacation," it is rare that we rest. We go someplace we've never been and load our days and nights with so many activities that we need a vacation just to recover from our vacation. Not to mention all the strange and different food and drink we consume in the name of fun and adventure while we are away.

Therefore, my research and experience with fasting have led me to believe that a fast is the exact *tune-up* our bodies so desperately and regularly need. Let me explain it from a medical perspective.

From the Medical Perspective

Early in my fasting journey, I happened upon a book entitled *Fasting and Eating for Health, A Medical Doctor's Program for Conquering Disease* by Joel Fuhrman, MD. In his book, Dr. Fuhrman chronicles his use of fasting in his medical practice to heal many conditions believed to be chronic, terminal, and without a known cure. This book became my go-to reference when I faced any illness. It was Dr. Fuhrman's discussion on fasting to heal fibroid tumors that encouraged my twenty-one-day fast now more than seventeen years ago. I had read this book many years prior to my encounter with Dr. Louise. If you remember from the introduction, Dr. Louise was my OBGYN who endorsed my belief in fasting as a cure for my own fibroids and encouraged me to share my experiences in this very book for women in similar positions.

Specifically, in reference to fasting, Dr. Fuhrman states:

> Therapeutic fasting accelerates the healing process and allows the body to recover from serious disease in a dramatically short period of time. In my practice, I have seen fasting eliminate lupus and arthritis, remove chronic skin conditions such as psoriasis and eczema, heal the digestive tract in patients with ulcerative colitis and Crohn's disease, and quickly eliminate cardiovascular diseases such as high blood pressure and angina. In these cases, the recoveries were permanent: fasting enabled long-time disease sufferers to unchain themselves from their multiple toxic drugs and even eliminate the need for surgery, which was recommended to some of them as their only solution.

Although I do not intend to repeat Dr. Fuhrman's book word for word, I will detail some of the issues he discusses in his first chapter, "Fasting for Physical Rejuvenation," that includes a discussion of the following topics: what fasting is; our natural human capacity to fast; the differences between fasting and starvation; how fasting restores the human body; the longstanding history of fasting; discomforts associated with fasting; the detoxification and improvement in organ function as a result of fasting, and how fasting typically achieves results where other methods have failed.

In chapters 2-10, Dr. Fuhrman's book discusses other issues that may be of concern to those contemplating a fast and worrying about the medical soundness of this process. Those chapters are:

2 Improper Nutrition;
3 Understanding Health and Disease;
4 Headaches and Hypoglycemia: Two Misunderstood Conditions;
5 The Road Back to a Healthy Heart;
6 Recovery from Diabetes Through Optimal Nutrition;
7 Autoimmune Disease: A Superior Approach;
8 Overweight and Other Chronic Medical Conditions Respond to Fasting;

9 A Chapter for Physicians and for Readers Who Want More Technical Information; and
10 What to Expect on Your First Fast.

Of particular importance and confirmation of God's hand on this process was Dr. Louise's admission that many doctors know that when they surgically remove the fibroids from a woman, that those tumors will then likely grow back. Nevertheless, the surgeries continue and affect not only women with fibroid tumors but those who live with and love them as well. It is one of the modern days "issue of blood"[7] referenced in the Bible, and now as in the biblical days, a supernatural intervention and a collision of grace and faith are needed to effect a cure.

I am a Doctor of Jurisprudence and not a medical doctor, and therefore, I do not purport to justify the biblically-based fasting that I write about with medical support. Rather, I find Dr. Fuhrman's writings, replete with case studies about the healing of so many different ailments, highly persuasive. If you are anything like me, you want to know about people who have done it before you and what level of success they were able to achieve. For those who have concerns about the medical soundness of fasting, I offer the writings of Dr. Fuhrman, referenced above. Trust me; I know how scary this sounds, especially if you have an illness that requires daily medication. By all means, do your own research and seek the help of a fasting professional to oversee and direct your journey. Also, know and expect that you most likely get "push back" from traditional physicians who know little or nothing of holistic remedies and will seek to scare you away from such tactics. In the end, the decision is yours.

The Importance of Elimination—We are What We Eat—Cancer Begins in the Colon

As a child, I remember that my mother's response to every complaint I had was the same: "When have you had a bowel movement?" Regardless of the malady, be it a stomachache, rash, headache, boil, or pimple, my mother's answer always pointed back to my bowels. It seemed impossible to me that one function of the body could be the answer to so many issues, but I now understand—she was right. Our bodies cannot function properly if our bowels are not moving on the regular.

Cancer and so many other diseases begin in the colon. I am sure you have heard this, and scientific research bears this out. The colon is the garbage dump of our bodies; it is where the waste from the foods from which our bodies have pulled the nutrients needed resides until a bowel movement forces the residue and waste out. The way this works is simple: The food we eat today pushes out the food we ate yesterday and the day before. But, how is this accomplished if we are not eating? And why is this important?

When we are not giving our bodies new food (i.e., we have turned down our plates to fast), our bodies will feed off stored fat contained in our tissue. As your body is forced to use this stored fat, you see immediate weight loss. More importantly, as your body processes this stored fat, it is also pulling out the stored toxins, poisons, and the root of the diseases that might be growing in your body. During a fast, it becomes even more important to push these poisons out of your systems less you get sick(er).

Because you are not eating new food that operates to push out the old food, you must somehow force a bowel movement. This can be accomplished in several different ways, including a natural laxative tea, a salt flush, or an enema.

Several laxative teas are readily available in the marketplace. Two of my favorites are Yogi brand "Get Regular" and Medicinal "Smooth Move." Both work well for me, but I caution that a cup of tea made the traditional way may prove too strong, so I use each tea bag twice:

on the first day, leaving it in hot water for several minutes and then on the second day allowing the tea bag to continue to brew. I usually drink the laxative tea at night, right before bedtime.

The laxative tea may be enough to force a bowel movement for some, but if not, you may follow the next morning with a salt flush. This is accomplished by drinking a quart of warm-hot water that contains two teaspoons of sea salt as rapidly as comfortable. Within the hour, you should experience a total cleanse. Sometimes I do this in the morning so that I am not waiting for the laxative to work and can get on with my day.

If, by the end of the day, for whatever reason (and every day is different), I have not had a bowel movement, I will give myself an enema. As important as a bowel movement is when you are not fasting, it becomes ten times more important when you are fasting for two reasons. I believe the first reason is that without regular (daily) bowel movements while fasting, you will get sick and could possibly die. Whether you are eating or not, your body continues to make waste, and you must push that waste out.

The second reason is, if not being forced to digest food, your body begins to perform preventive or corrective maintenance. God designed our bodies to heal themselves, and fasting gives this function time to work at the highest level. White blood cells and red blood cells rush to the site of inflammation and dysfunction; body levels such as blood pressure and blood sugar are readjusted; new healthy cells are generated as poisons and toxins are pulled from the tissue and blood released from the body in the form of urine and bowel. It, therefore, becomes even more necessary to push out these germs and diseases that our bodies are attacking, killing, and attempting to remove during the fast.

Fasting removes old waste that may have been in our bodies for years. I am sure you have heard horror stories about how many of us are carrying around waste-containing food we ate years ago. This is especially true if we have a distended belly and are morbidly obese. This old undigested or partially digested food is hanging around in our colon and potentially making us sick. Our colon is approximately five feet long. A normal healthy bowel movement should be softly formed, brownish in color, and of substantial length.

If you are only consuming liquids, your bowel movements will be largely liquid. If we consume large amounts of fruits and vegetables, our poop will smell like fruit and vegetables, as these foods tend to move through our system quickly. If we consume products like chicken and fish, our poop is more odorific due in part to the length of time it takes our bodies to digest this type of food. The elimination of pork and beef smells really bad because it takes our bodies so long to break this type of food down while it is literally dead and rotting in our body. It may, in a healthy body, remain in the digestive tract for two-three days, and in an unhealthy body, for years.

This fact forms the basis for the reason so many people periodically perform a cleanse. Although not a full-blown fast, people will modify their diet to increase their intake of fruits and vegetables, increase their water and take any number of supplements designed to increase their bowel movements. This modified fast is designed to cleanse the body of excess waste, poisons, and toxins by cleaning the stored waste in the tissue, bloodstream, and colon.

Many people opt to precede their fast with a cleanse. Others believe this is easier to accomplish by removing themselves from their normal home environment and going to a spa, where their meals are prepared, the ability to cheat is removed, and or their fast is monitored by a professional/medical team. I have not yet had that luxury, but understand that I find fasting almost easy and have no issue going about the regular activities of my day without eating. Knowing the beauty and benefit of the fast and having experienced the faster's high (similar to the runner's high), it is not usually a problem to get through the first day or two of the fast when you are missing food.

As every fast is not the same, sometimes you will begin a fast and just not be able to make it through to completion, however long that may be. Accept the fact that it's not a good time, move on, and try it again next week, next month, or next year. Whatever you do, do not stress over what you may perceive as a failed attempt. Fasting is a discipline that takes time to develop. And fasting as a healing art may require two, three, or four efforts. You may even find that you have been unable to reach a total cure, but by fasting once a month, you are able to manage your medical condition or achieve whatever result you are pursuing. Whatever the goal, elimination will play an important role in that process.

What to Expect While Fasting

Everyone's experience with fasting is different. You will even find that there are differences within each fast that a single person undertakes. The more you fast, the more you will become aware of your body, your particular needs and responses to going without food. The more you fast, the easier it becomes, especially once you have realized a victory or two and celebrated the healing, weight loss, clear skin, and other benefits (you may no longer need medication for high blood pressure or diabetes) that are the result of previous fasts. Please know that I am not suggesting that anyone abandon their medications. *If you are on medications for any health condition, I strongly suggest you undertake a fast only under the supervision of a doctor, who can monitor your condition and gradually wean you off the prescribed medications.*

Although everyone's experience may be different, here are some things you might experience that seem daunting at first, but quickly turn into only a minor inconvenience. Common problems you might experience during a fast include:

Hunger

Where is the surprise here? An overwhelming sense of hunger that comes and goes during the fast, especially in the first few days, is to be expected. This is where discipline comes in. Having prepared yourself mentally for the fasting experience is also critical. Fasting, or denying oneself food for a period, like breaking any other habit, requires mind over matter, at least at first. If you have ever tried to give up anything else, like sugar, meat, cigarettes, or alcohol, to name a few, you will remember that the first few days were the hardest. I remember when I was trying to quit smoking some forty years ago[8], hearing that the physical part of the addiction was gone within three days. Thereafter it was a mental craving, which required the retraining of the mind to no longer think a cigarette was needed or wanted, that it was pleasant, cool, or good for you.

Fasting experts suggest that there is more going on than just your body craving food. Rather, feeling hungry is a natural consequence of the time it takes for your body to shift from food intake into fat-burning mode. Arguably, once your body gets the message that it should pull energy from the fat stored in your body, it ceases to demand food (i.e., make you feel hungry). Like battling any other addiction, this period generally lasts only the first one to three days. Also, it gives me comfort to know that, unlike other addictions that I might want to get rid of forever, my fast from food is only a temporary period of abstinence, and I will eventually eat again.

During the fast, I take particular pleasure in planning some of those meals I will eat upon returning to food, which are always extremely healthy and full of good things like vegetables and fruits and whole grains. Interestingly, it is not the ice cream, cake, brownies, wine, or a juicy steak that I crave while fasting, but beautiful colorful plates of vegetables and fish and chicken and beans. Go figure. In a clean state, my body craves and makes clean, healthy food choices. But when I am overweight and my blood levels are off, I crave more of what got me there. As I write this, I begin to think that during a fast, not only is your body undergoing a transformative healing, but so is your mind. After all, do you really want to spend from ten to twenty-one days (the time it takes for a healing in your body) without food, enjoy the renewed body, devoid of fifteen to thirty pounds, clearer skin, freedom from medicines you required which were filled with chemicals and their companion side effects, and then rush back to your old habits and food choices that got you to the point of needing a fast in the first place? I hope not.

Unlike the hunger you feel when you are eating, this hunger does not build and build but rather floats in and out and is, in my opinion, mild. A drink of water or tea will normally relieve this sensation. One of the benefits of the lemonade discussed previously is that periodic sipping on this beverage eliminates the hunger sensation altogether and certainly quashes it when it comes. To me, a feeling of hunger is an indication that it is time to take in some fluid.

Headaches

Another common problem you might experience while fasting is a headache. This may be brought on by any number of things, but probably the most likely one is a need for fluid. I have heard that headaches, in general, are the result of dehydration. We take an aspirin or other pain killer and use water to wash it down. We believe it was the pain killer that brought about the relief, but in actuality, it was the water that cured the headache because we were dehydrated. The problem is dehydration; the symptom is the headache. We choose to treat the symptom rather than the problem. In the fasting mode, I would never choose to take a pain killer because it is a chemical, the likes of which you are by fasting seeking to eliminate from your system.

Another cause of a headache might likely be the need for elimination, which is, in my opinion, once again, critical during a fast. Even though you are not taking in food, your body is feeding off stored fat and processing it as food, and therefore it is making waste, which must be removed from your body, or *you will get sick*. Although there are some who disagree with me, I believe that you should go every day and during a fast; as discussed in the chapter on elimination, most people must take a deliberate action to make this happen. Some people have regular metabolism and regular bowel movements regardless. I had a friend back during the 1980s who said a laxative was not required for him, even during a fast, because all he had to do was drink a glass of water, and he would have a bowel movement. As I finish this writing with a twenty-one-day fast, I switched to a total fast with only distilled water. Much to my surprise, I had a natural bowel movement every morning after a cup of warm water. Who knew?

Light-Headedness

Not surprisingly, some people have a "spaced-out" or lightheaded feeling. This is not a reaction I have felt on any kind of regular basis. On the few times when I did feel lightheaded, the intake of fluid would generally alleviate the feeling. Some suggest a salty drink as a remedy for light-headedness. I caution you that a few people may faint, so a feeling of light-headedness should immediately cause you to sit or lay down, preferably on the ground, until the feeling passes. This will eliminate your ability for injury should you pass out. I should reiterate, I have never come anywhere near fainting, even on my forty-day fasts.

Intense Cold

The feeling of intense cold might also be an issue. Because of this sensation, I learned how quickly our bodies are affected by what we eat and drink. My first long-term fasts, as near as I can recall, occurred during the winter. I live in Chicago, which is known for its brutal winter weather. I remember more than one occasion when I fasted in January with subzero temperatures. On one occasion, I did a lot of outdoor walking and taking public transportation. Surprisingly, I was not bothered by the cold (I am a Chicago native). But on those rare occasions when I did catch a chill, a cup of warm liquid, tea, heated lemonade, or even warm water would quickly adjust my body temperature. And on the flip side, I have learned that cold beverages can quickly cool me off when I am overheated. Neither the hot nor the cold beverages work nearly as quickly when I am eating as they do while I am fasting.

Extreme Fatigue

Fasting, in general, is best accomplished with more rest than you might normally require. A total fast done under the supervision of a physician will generally have you retreat to a facility for total rest during the fast, with regular observations of your blood and vitamin levels. I have never had this luxury. Although I do find that I am fatigued on certain days, I actually get more done during a fast. I set goals to get things done that have been hanging around forever and generally achieve those goals. I think that I am different from many people in my energy for work and constant activity. At least at first, you should probably plan to do as little as possible and rest as much as possible. After all, your body is performing an immense project of overall healing. You should not stress yourself out during this time with work, let alone more work. Allowing your body to rest is probably the best advice since you are placing yourself in a mode of intense healing and should govern yourself accordingly. If you were in the hospital, most of your time would be spent in a prone position in bed, resting if not asleep, and certainly not performing copious amounts of work.

Bad Breath, Chapped Lips, and a Coated Tongue

Your breath will/may stink, and your lips may/will become chapped. I suspect this is because your body is unearthing and breaking down fat and partially digested food that you may have been carrying around for years, so not unlike any other garbage dump, it smells when disturbed. Truth is, I don't know why, but it does, so just deal with it. Use mouthwash regularly, buy a Chapstick and move on. Do not, however, decide you need a peppermint: that is cheating. You may also notice that your tongue is coated with a white substance. Wipe it off with a washcloth.

Flatulence and Poop

By all means, do not think you can pass a little gas. It will be most likely be liquid, and you will be highly embarrassed. Any desire to pass gas should send you immediately to the toilet. Finally, your poop will smell... awfully bad. Remember, your body is pulling waste from stored and partially digested food that you may have been housing for twenty years. It is putrid, but thank God it is coming out of your system, where it is making you sick and killing you. So, unless you live alone, be kind to your family. Use the bathroom fan and spray air freshener because right now, your elimination is not pleasant. As if it ever was?

On another note, I was raised by a nurse, and nurses don't mince words. They say exactly what they mean and are not in any way embarrassed by regular bodily functions. First and foremost, they worship the holiness of bowel movements, and they talk about it freely and regularly (pun intended). During this fast, you should take on a relationship with your poop unlike you have ever known. It is critical to watch your elimination. This sounds weird, but you need to know what is coming out of your body and how it is changing throughout the fast. Observing your poop even when you are not fasting is important as it can be an indication of your health or the lack thereof. We all know that diarrhea and constipation both indicate an imbalance within your system. And a change in the color, texture, or amount of your poop could indicate internal bleeding. However, it may just be an indication of what you have eaten (beets, for instance, will make your poop dark) or a reaction to a vitamin (like iron supplements).

I remember one fast where I started with the intention of doing fourteen days. But around day thirteen, my elimination changed so drastically; I believed that I had uncovered a disease or something horrific growing within me. My poop changed in color, texture, and smell. The change was so drastic that I continued my fast for another seven days, wanting to rid my system of whatever had been uncovered because although I didn't know what it was, I felt it was not good, and I needed to get all of it out of my body. So, I say this in all seriousness: look at your poop before you flush it. It will tell you things about what is going on inside of you better than a stethoscope or X-ray machine. Learn your body and listen to what it is telling you.

You may also experience diarrhea on the first few days after you break your fast as your body returns to the normal digestion of food, especially if you return to eating heavy items, starches, meats, and sugar too rapidly. Find out more about that in the chapter about breaking the fast.

The Good Things

I have told you about the possible side effects that you may encounter so that you will not be frightened if you experience any of them. On the flip side of that coin are a number of good side effects and benefits you might also notice.

Deeper Sleep and Better Rest

I am an Olympic sleeper whose rest is almost never disturbed. Nevertheless, I notice that I sleep like a baby during a fast, and not the one with colic. I fall asleep quickly, sleep the night through, and awake early, feeling refreshed and well-rested. A nap during the day produces the same kind of intense sleep and total refreshing.

Watch that Belly Shrink!

One of my greatest joys is watching the transformation of my body, especially the removal of belly fat and the shrinking waistline. And I do the thing you are most times told not to do. I weigh myself every morning because weight loss is usually one of my goals. To see the weight drop is very encouraging as I inch toward one of my goals, pound after pound.

Excess weight will come off only where needed. Unlike diets that may leave you with sunken cheeks and a gaunt face because of a rapid weight loss, I have never had this experience, even after a forty-day fast. Rather your body appears to go straight to the problem area where the excess fat lies and remove it.

Your Skin Will Clear and Become Radiant

One of my favorite aspects of fasting is the difference in how you will look. You will notice that many of the eruptions you may have seen on your face will disappear. I have noticed dark splotches on my face dry up, break apart, and fall off. A radiance, a glow, if you will, invades your skin, and you will take on a look of healthiness that not only will you notice, but other people will see too. They will undoubtedly comment on it because it is a phenomenal transformation. It comes from a place of peace and healing, and it shows on your face.

Area of Inflammation Resolve

Arthritis and other areas of inflammation in your bones and joints may well reduce and/or totally resolve. This will improve your movement as you alleviate the pain you have felt for years. I also understand that the resolution of osteoporosis is a benefit you might experience. I sometimes experience low back pain and pain in my ankle as a result of spraining it a year ago. Today at the nail salon, I had my eyebrows arched, which requires me to lay down on a table. When the technician is done, she usually has to offer her arm to pull me up. Today after completing a twenty-day fast, nineteen pounds lighter and pain-free, I literally jumped up with no assistance, feeling like a young girl!

Get in Tune with Your Body

As I have said before, God designed our bodies with the ability to heal themselves, but we never give them a chance. One of the wonders of fasting is to watch how your body responds to what you are doing. It is like every fiber of your being is applauding your journey, such that you know, innately, that you are doing something good. The overwhelming sense of accomplishment, discipline, and healing is unmistakable. You will feel like you are entering a new space, a space where anything is possible. A space where you fall deeper in love with yourself and want to do what is good for your health. A space where you will hear that still small voice talking to you, and it is not scary or frightening but comforting. Many have described this space as akin to a runner's high. Suffice it to say, it is a special and privileged space few people get to enter. A space where you might want to stay awhile and revisit from time to time. A place where God becomes more real and where you feel His presence, like never before.

Develop a Different Attitude About Food

Almost every illness or condition we experience is the result of poor dietary habits. Obesity, diabetes, high blood pressure, a heart condition, arthritis, gout, autoimmune diseases, sinus problems, and even asthma are the result of poor dietary choices and/or excessive eating. Although a long-term fast may get you to a point of healing, a healthy, restructured dietary plan is what will keep you there. I suspect that many people are reading this book because they are sick and tired of being sick and tired. To believe that you can return to your old ways of excessive eating and eating the wrong kinds of foods is ludicrous since these are the things that got you where you are in the first place, in need of a divine intervention. Going without food for ten or twenty days shows you how you can be in charge of food cravings and be disciplined at a level you didn't know you had.

A Deeper Dive into Your Relationship with God

As previously said, fasting was created by God as a tool to be used in tough times. Nothing pleases God more than when we seek His guidance and rely upon

His Word. The Bible is filled with what I call *if-thens. If* we do this, *then* He will do that. I have learned and now fully believe that even if I get it wrong, if I am stepping out on faith and doing what I believe God is leading me to do, He then will honor my faith. He will protect me, guide me and direct me. I, therefore, have no fear of taking on the adventure of a faith-based fast.

How to Break a Fast

This chapter is probably one of the most important you will read in this book. Break the fast slowly, especially if it has been a long-term fast. Conventional wisdom says that you should take as many days to return to normal eating as you have fasted. I never do.

I always break my fast the same way: with an orange. If oranges are not your favorite fruit, you might choose another fruit, but I have never had a bad reaction to an orange.

The worst thing you can do is to drop a big heavy meal into a system that has only had liquids for days, weeks, or maybe even a month or more. Return to food slowly, continuing the intake of fluids, choosing those foods in their natural state, or softly cooked, easy-to-digest vegetables, avoiding heavy salt, starch, and sugar.

When you are ready to add protein, go with chicken or fish.

I make a vegetable soup as one of my fast-breaking meals. The soup is homemade and includes onions, garlic, new potatoes, broccoli, carrots, zucchini, and natural seasonings. It is tasty, soothing, and goes down easily.

I also find that returning to food after a long-term fast is often accompanied by diarrhea. A round of probiotics will clear this up, but it will take time to return to normal eating.

Be patient.

Epilogue

Doing what God has assigned is rarely easy. Writing this book is no exception: it has been a labor. I knew that I had to do it: that fact was confirmed so many times by so many seemingly unconnected people, not to mention that still small voice that just wouldn't let me be. But getting it done was no easy task and not being able to get it done was equally hard.

It never occurred to me in all my years of fasting that God had an ulterior motive for constantly leading me along this path. I did come to realize that there was something different about my ability to turn my plate down so frequently, as friends and family would look at me and say the all too familiar, "Girl, you fasting again?" But what a privilege and an honor I now feel to know that God was up to something bigger than me. Bigger even than my extreme good health with which I am blessed, including being healed from several conditions that are believed to have no cures. And I will forever credit fasting with the delayed and yet uneventful pregnancies that brought to life my two darlings while I was deep within the throes of middle age, long past what conventional wisdom formerly believes to be a safe time to bear children.

As I struggled over the past two years to get this book completed, I realized that God did some special things for me with great purpose. A large part of this purpose was to share with others, likeminded and skeptics, what He's done. The fact that He has a way, a plan, a supernatural and yet so natural design for our healing. Can you imagine a manufacturer who made a machine but has no idea how to fix it when it breaks down? That's not true in the natural, and it's not true in the spiritual either.

God made us: we know that for certain, and as our Creator, He knows everything about us and how to repair and replace our brokenness. Won't you give His formula a try? Just turn your plate down for a moment and let God be God. When you decide to fast for healing, you are letting God know that you trust Him to repair your body, His creation and that you have enough faith to follow His plan, set forth in His Word. Focus on God in the process and lean not to your own understanding, trusting in God with all of your heart.

About the Author

Calvita J. Frederick is a native Chicagoan and graduate of Chicago Public Schools. She attended John Marshall Harlan High School, located on the city's far southside. In addition to her studies, Calvita had (and still has!) a love for fashion and modeling. She was the first visibly African American model on the Montgomery Wards' Pacesetter Teen Board, and in addition to appearing in fashion shows around the city, Calvita was chosen numerous times to appear as a teen model in the Chicago Tribune.

After graduating high school, Calvita went on to attend Eureka College in Eureka, Illinois. During her time there, she continued to model on the Marshall Fields' College Board, pledged Alpha Kappa Alpha sorority, and graduated cum laude.

Calvita continued her studies at the prestigious Howard University School of Law, where she graduated, *Law Review*, and received one of the highest paying jobs for law graduates in 1978, staff attorney for Ford Motor Company, located in Dearborn, Michigan.

In 1982, she returned to Chicago and started Calvita J. Frederick and Associates, Attorneys at Law, a general civil practice law firm where she obtained her highest paying settlements in cases against Chrysler Corporation and Aon Corporation. In 1988, Calvita expanded her talents once again and became a licensed real estate broker.

After more than twenty years as a practicing lawyer, Calvita decided to follow her faith and her heart by looking for a more calming and peaceful profession. She never dreamed that preparing her secret blends of tea for family and friends would turn into a full-time career, but that's exactly what happened. After continually receiving encouragement to market her teas, Calvita took the plunge and launched Magnolia Spice Teas in 1998. Known for their distinctive homemade taste and all-natural ingredients, Magnolia's healthy beverages have received awards (1st Place Best Ready-to-Drink Sweet Tea 2005 World Tea Expo, Las Vegas) and recognition and kudos from beverage industry, trade, and business publications alike, including *BevNet, Beverage Aisle, Tea and Coffee, Black Enterprise* and the *Chicago Defender, Chicago Tribune and Chicago Sun Times.*

In 2008, Calvita returned full time to the practice of law and currently focuses her law practice on cases alleging discrimination in employment (based upon race, sex, age, and disability), nursing home abuse, probate, real estate, and family law. Victories include cases against Blue Cross/Blue Shield, Sodexo Operations, LLC., Kaufman Hall, Chrysler Corporation, Allstate Insurance Co., Chicago Transit Authority, Renaissance Park South Nursing and Living Center, Holy Cross Hospital, E*Trade Bank, Tishmah Speyer, US Bank, PepsiCo, Lake Forest Academy, Jones, Lang Lasalle, Rock Valley College, Fidelity National Information Services a/k/a Sunguard, Churchview Supportive Services, Gardant Management Solutions, Carson Pierre Scott, and Cintas, to name a few. More information regarding her legal practice can be found at: *www.cjfredericklaw.com.*

Calvita is the divorced mother of two adult daughters, Samantha and Simone, and an active member of the Apostolic Church of God. Her advice is to seek God first and fearlessly follow the dream He places in your heart.

Appendix

The Lemonade Ingredients: Lemons, Limes, Maple Syrup, And Cayenne Pepper

It is no surprise that the drink chosen to sustain one on the Master Cleanse includes lemons or limes, maple syrup, and cayenne pepper. When undertaking a fast for healing, this lemonade is a perfect liquid companion to fight whatever is ailing you. Although water is best, this lemonade runs a close second for the best way to get hydration during a fast. In the case of these ingredients, we often see them as mere toppings, seasonings, and garnishes, leaving their immense benefits to the health of our bodies often overlooked. Though it would be onerous to give an exhaustive account of lemons, limes, maple syrup, and cayenne pepper, in the space of this section, I offer a list of particularly relevant benefits and beyond.

Lemons and Limes

Tiny in size, lemons and limes are packed full of healthful properties. Though we often use the flesh and juice of these colorful and acidic fruits, their skin is beneficial as well. Arguably, lemons and limes contain so much nutritional value that they demand your attention as a dietary staple.

An Immune Booster

Both tart and tasty, lemons and limes are packed with Vitamin C, a powerful immune booster the body needs but does not produce on its own. Commonly understood to decrease the duration of the common cold, Vitamin C attacks virus cells and kills bacteria.[9]

An Assistant with Asthma

Lemon juice has the distinct ability to both treat and prevent asthma. This is due to the high concentrations of Vitamin C and antioxidants contained in lemons. It has been proposed that vitamin C can reduce the stress placed on airway tissues which, in turn, may reduce their hypersensitivity to common asthma triggers. Lemons are also believed to help the lungs breathe easier and to strengthen the body to lessen asthma attacks.

An Iron Absorption Facilitator

Iron is a precious mineral required by our bodies to help the blood carry oxygen to the cells and produces energy for regular cell function. Our body's absorption of iron is facilitated by citric acid and vitamin C, found in high levels in both lemons and limes.

An Assistant with Cancer

Lemon peels contain a high dosage of a terpene called d-limonene. Terpenes are aromatic compounds commonly found in many plants. In lab studies with animals, d-limonene had a considerable positive effect on cancer cells.[10] More recently, in a study of a group of forty-three women with operable breast cancer, those given two grams of limonene daily showed a 22 percent reduction in the expression of tumor markers.[11] Another study linked citrus peels to a reduced risk of cancerous skin cells.[12]

To Improve Complexion

Lemons, limes, and oranges all contain collagen, a nutrient known to aid in achieving youthful-looking and wrinkle-free skin. Collagen is believed to delay the aging process and tighten your skin. The vitamin C present in citrus also naturally brightens skin with regular intake.

Lowers Risk of Stroke and Lowers Blood Pressure

A study found that an ingredient in citrus fruit called auraptene lowers blood pressure in rodents bred with hypertension. Lemons are an age-old staple of eastern medicine, which prizes them for keeping blood vessels soft and pliable, which reduces blood pressure.[13]

Assists Nervous System

Lemons and limes (not just bananas) are high in potassium, which is crucial to nervous system health. Low levels of potassium in the blood are believed to cause anxiety and depression. The nervous system also needs an adequate amount of potassium to send sustainable signals to the heart.

Highly Alkalizing

Citrus fruits are acidic outside of the body. But once they are fully metabolized, the lemon/lime's minerals are dissociated in the bloodstream. This raises the pH of body tissue above seven, making the body more alkaline, the favored state. A recent article discusses the benefits of maintaining your body in an alkaline condition. Those benefits include: slowing the development of osteoporosis, keeping the heart healthy, encouraging better digestion, preventing arthritis; boosting the immune system and the brain; promoting better sleep; and improving metabolic acidosis.[14]

A Powerful Anti-Viral and Anti-Inflammatory

Lemon and lime juice are proven to be both antibacterial and antiviral. These fruits have powerful antiviral properties on the mucous membranes in the nose and throat when ill and boost the immune system internally. For centuries, people have used lemon juice to speed up the recovery from canker sores. In addition, the fruits' anti-inflammatory properties help fight respiratory tract infections, sore throats, and inflammation of the tonsils.

Helps Relieve Constipation

The citric acid in limes and lemons aid with digestion because it interacts with other enzymes and acids, which stimulate the secretion of gastric juice and promote digestion. Lemon essential oil is slightly different than lemon juice and is a much more concentrated version that has long been touted as an alternative medicine, especially used with digestion and constipation. The bile production that lemon induces can also increase intestinal peristalsis.

Whether fasting or eating, because of the numerous benefits listed above, which list is not exhaustive, it is obvious that lemons and limes should top the list when grocery shopping.

Maple Syrup: A Powerhouse Collection of Minerals and Vitamins

Maple syrup, although relatively low in calories, contains a concentration of minerals and vitamins, unlike many other sweeteners. It is rich in essential trace minerals, including manganese, zinc, iron, and copper, nutrients needed in small quantities but not naturally produced by our bodies. Maple syrup also contains calcium, phosphorus, magnesium, sodium, zinc, and potassium in terms of minerals. It also offers the vitamins such as riboflavin, thiamin, Vitamin B6, and niacin.

Health Benefits of Maple Syrup

Maple syrup offers various antioxidants, which used in moderate amounts, helps to lower inflammation, maintains blood sugar levels, and provides various nutrients necessary for good health. In comparison to honey, maple syrup contains a low number of calories as compared to a high amount of minerals and vitamins that help support heart health and enhance the immune system.[15]

Antioxidant Activity

Maple syrup has antioxidants that are needed for the good health. The antioxidant properties found in Maple syrup help to eliminate free radicals that are the main cause for health ailments.

Heart Health

Maple syrup is essential for the heart health and is believed to prevent atherosclerosis, stroke, and cardiovascular ailments. Zinc, one of the ingredients contained in maple syrup, is effective in preventing these health conditions and enhancing cell functions. The low content of zinc naturally found in our bodies can lead to high chances of injuries and affect the heart functions.[16]

Reproductive Health

The intake of Maple syrup may maintain the reproductive health of males. The minerals such as zinc are essential for maintaining the health of the prostate gland. The low amount of zinc and other minerals naturally found in our bodies may increase the chances of the development of prostate cancer. *Id.*

Strengthen Immunity

Maple syrup is an excellent source of magnesium and zinc, which are vital for the immune system. Manganese and zinc are essential for increasing the white blood cells that enhance the immunity power of the body. The healthy supplementation of these minerals through the use of Maple Syrup helps in restoration of the levels of magnesium and zinc.

Treat Arthritis

It is believed that certain inflammatory diseases, such as arthritis, could be cured with Maple syrup because it has quebecol, which provides anti-inflammatory properties.

Cayenne Pepper

Cayenne pepper has a long history of therapeutic use in many cultures, including those of the Americas and China. As a powerful compound with many uses, Cayenne pepper is currently gaining popularity for its cleansing and detoxifying properties, along with its ability to stimulate circulation and neutralize acidity. In addition, Cayenne pepper contains many other benefits.

Anti-Irritant Properties

Our bodies become irritated for any number of reasons, including diet, illness, stress, and environmental toxins. Known as a fiery spice, ironically, cayenne can help "put out the fire" and ease an upset stomach, sore throats, coughs, and occasional diarrhea.[17]

Clears Congestion

Cayenne pepper aids in breaking up and moving congested mucus, which can assist those suffering from a stuffed-up nose or sinuses due to allergies or seasonal illnesses.[18]

Soothes Occasional Joint Discomfort

Capsaicin, a substance found in high, is believed to send chemical messengers from the skin into the joint, offering relief for occasional joint discomfort.[19] For this reason, many people with stiff, sore joints use creams and lotion that contain cayenne.

Helps Preserve Food

Cayenne is an excellent preservative and has been used traditionally to prevent food contamination from bacteria.[20]

Promotes Longevity

A study using data collected from almost half a million people found that those who ate spicy foods had a 14 percent chance of living longer than those that didn't. Researchers also found that regular consumption of chili peppers aligned with reduced rates of death from respiratory disease, heart problems, and cancer.[21]

Promotes Heart Health

Animal studies found that capsaicin reduced serious heart arrhythmias and improved cardiac blood flow.[22]

Other Benefits

Cayenne Pepper is also believed to encourage healthy body weight by decreasing the appetite, leading to less caloric intake throughout the day, and increasing the metabolism, which aids the body in burning excess fat.[23] When applied directly to the site, cayenne may help ease the discomfort associated with a sore tooth. As a topical remedy or poultice, cayenne has been used to treat snake bites, rheumatism, sores, wounds, and lumbago or lower back discomfort. Finally, many people find that a dash cayenne can add a little delicious zest to otherwise bland food.[24]

Bibliography

Health Fitness Revolution. "Top 10 Health Benefits of Lemon and Limes." Last modified September 15, 2020. https://www.healthfitnessrevolution.com/top-10-health-benefits-of-lemons-and-limes/

Health Benefits Times. "Maple Syrup Facts and Benefits." Accessed August 4, 2019. https://www.healthbenefit-stimes.com/maple-syrup-facts-and-benefits/

Global Healing. "17 Health Benefits of Cayenne Pepper." Dr. Edward Group. Last modified October 21, 2015. https://globalhealingcenter.com/natural-health

Endnotes

1 I do not have diabetes even though I carry the gene. However, my maternal grandmother, mother, father, and sister have all been diagnosed with the diabetes.

2 Mize, J. (1993). *Supernatural Childbirth: Experiencing the Promises of God Concerning Conception and Delivery* (Illustrated edition). Harrison House Publishers.

3 As Plaintiff's counsel I have won and or settled cases against Chrysler Corporation, AON Corporation, PepsiCo, Sodexo, US Foods, Chicago Transit Authority, Jones, Lang LaSalle, Kaufman Hall, Tishman Speyer and SunGard Trading Services, Inc.

4 Brandhorst S, Choi IY, Wei M, Cheng CW, Sedrakyan S, Navarrete G, Dubeau L, Yap LP, Park R, Vinciguerra M, Di Biase S, Mirzaei H, Mirisola MG, Childress P, Ji L, A Periodic Diet that Mimics Fasting Promotes Multi-System Regeneration, Enhanced Cognitive Performance, and Healthspan. Groshen S, Penna F, Odetti P, Perin L, Conti PS, Ikeno Y, Kennedy BK, Cohen P, Morgan TE, Dorff TB, Longo VD. Cell Metab. 2015 Jul 7;22(1):86-99. doi: 10.1016/j.cmet.2015.05.012. Epub 2015 Jun 18.

PMID: 26094889; PMCID: PMC4509734.

5 NY Times, "Intermittent Fasting Made my Life Easier and Happier."

6 NY Times, "Intermittent Fasting Made my Life Easier and Happier."

7 Another is polycystic ovarian disorder.

8 I began smoking in college and never really enjoyed it but kept it up for some eight or nine years. In high school when my girlfriends were smoking weed, I could get high off a Salem, so there was no need to smoke marijuana. Besides, marijuana was a real drug and I was a good girl. It is interesting to note that in order to become a smoker, I had to fight through the high and nausea I experienced those first few weeks before I finally became addicted, and for some stupid reason, fight I did. I smoked Eve cigarettes because they were pretty and had flowers on them. I always had to keep the windows open, even in winter, because I couldn't stand the smell of cigarette smoke. Somewhere along the line I heard that if you smoked less than ten years, and quit, all damage done to your body from the tobacco and fire you breathed in would reverse itself. So, I began a journey to quit in year eight and between years eight and ten, I quit smoking eighteen times. It finally stuck, right before I reached the tenth year. But, once again, I digress.

9 Ströhle, A., & Hahn, A. (2009). Vitamin C und Immunfunktion [Vitamin C and immune function]. *Medizinische Monatsschrift fur Pharmazeuten*, 32(2), 49–56.

10S. Nikfar, A.F. Behboudi, in *Encyclopedia of Toxicology*

(Third Edition), 2014

11 Miller JA, Lang JE, Ley M, et al. Human breast tissue disposition and bioactivity of limonene in women with early-stage breast cancer. *Cancer Prev Res (Phila)*. 2013;6(6):577-584. doi:10.1158/1940-6207.CAPR-12-0452.

12 Hakim, I. A., Harris, R. B., & Ritenbaugh, C. (2000). Citrus peel use is associated with reduced risk of squamous cell carcinoma of the skin. *Nutrition and Cancer,* 37(2), 161–168. https://doi.org/10.1207/S15327914NC372_7.

13 Kennedy Club Fitness: 2018May Top 10 Health Benefits of Lemons and Limes.

14 Health Fitness Revolution - September 5, 2019.

15 www.internationalmaplesyrupinstitute.com

16 Little PJ, Bhattacharya R, Moreyra AE, Korichneva IL. Zinc and cardiovascular disease. *Nutrition*. 2010 Nov-Dec;26(11-12):1050-7. doi: 10.1016/j.nut.2010.03.007. PMID: 20950764.

17 Updated Oct 21, 2015, 17 *Health Benefits of Cayenne Pepper,* by Dr. Edward Group.

18 Ibid.

19 Ibid.

20 Ibid.

21 Ibid.

22 Ibid.

23 Ibid.

24 Ibid.

CPSIA information can be obtained
at www.ICGtesting.com
Printed in the USA
BVHW070450301121
622779BV00008B/499